SLIPSTREAM

Slipstream

KRISTYN J. SAUNDERS

WALLEAH PRESS

First published 2025
Walleah Press
South Launceston,
Tasmania, Australia 7249

www.walleahpress.com.au

Cover & Internal Design by Susan Le
Typeset in Sofia pro regular 9.5pt/14pt

A catalogue record for this book is available from the
National Library of Australia.

ISBN: 9781763825963

WALLEAH PRESS

For Lee

Agnes Martin said her paintings were for people to look at *before daily care strikes*. Suppose reading and writing do their best work *after daily care has struck* (and struck hard).

—C.D. Wright

CONTENTS

Each line is the mother's line.

The mother's child is in
a hospital.

(The difficult world has hurt the child.
The child has hurt herself.
The child is hurt.)

The lines are made
in the child's slip
stream.

_it's_

          not
          a room
          just
          a bed with
          curtains a
          round
          _it_

she

          messaged she's
          sorry she
          missed
          your
          call

for

          the lights
          through the
          night **_all_** _she_
          was allowed was
          a face washer
          to put over
          her **_eyes_**

LISTING

like split-flap display
the old white-on-
black electro-

mechanical information boards
for trains planes & buses,
metallic minutes click-

clacking one over
another after
next arrival for

next departure
for the late
the on time

the all aboard
the delay day-break
to day-fall, flat

anthem of the terminus,
early-autumn to mid-summer
terror daydreaming

past amber-lit readings
of *Click, Clack, Moo*
googly-eyed pages of *Cows*

That Type, the quiet street wandering
loose-limbed clarity
of mothers babies & old men,

cut flowers in metal buckets
apples in wooden bins,
through the drifting neural brace

of what might declare itself
next, rooms of undrawn blinds
room where streetlight limns

a small square window
of shelved books, long thin
slats of light brush

curve the ceiling, swing
shifts suspended, just–
grown child alive

grants license to worry
the metrics,
plot symptoms by

diagnoses
by medications by
outcomes, indexed

degrees of loss,
dawn recitation
a rough braid

of hand-holds
one over
the other over

sorrowful, careful,
it's too early,
or too late to be

a problem of safety
plans, scales
of intent, to be

a question of composition,
or trespass,
the post-Solari

sound an electronically-
generated flapping noise
to cue listeners

with updates
off page, their granular
traces turn

again, turnings
incommensurate, agglut-
inate annunciations

of what you more
or less dread, all
pinging sounds off

for the watch,
proximate places fixed,
alphanumeric scroll

piecemeal, fitful
consecution
backlit, silent

counter-attack
click clack quack
clickety, clack, quack

it's

not

a room

just

a bed

with curtains around it

she's

got

to stop *using*

the phone she

texted

the battery

is going

down

the nurses

can't help

during hand

over

she's

sorry

she missed your

call

he

seemed nice

the doctor

she hopes he's

good

all

she

was allowed

was a face washer

to *put over her*

eyes no

she's

not
sleeping
even
with extra

———

the

doc**to**r
she doesn't
know when
he's coming in
today
the nurse
messaged him

sorry

she missed
your call

better

than
the ER
bed

she

doesn**'t**
kn**o**w
if maybe she
shouldn't
bother she
doesn't know
at all

you

remember that
list they
forgot

to take
her shoelaces
she walked in ate
lunch sat
on the couch **all**
with shoelaces then
said
to the student nurse Um
I think **you need**
to take
these

————

the

high
risk patients
she's with
seem more like
high risk
of falling like
little
old
ladies

decreasing
———— to see if that
helps with ————
because sometimes
he said it can
make ————
worse
and

the high-

risk
patients she's with
seem more like
*high risk **of** falling like*
little old ladies

no

she can't
she's not
*al**lo**wed*
pens
or pencils
un
*super**vis**ed*

she is

not
allowed
pens or pencils
unsupervised
she can't

IN QUICK SUCCESSION

Pitched high
In the bend's dark clutch of tall
Trees, a loud sizzling crackle.

Fistfuls fall to the downhill
Slope and vanish

Into undergrowth, another
Thwack & then
Again.

Cones scattered ahead
On the path fallen grass
Green and segments sealed.

An umbrellaed elderly woman
Passes by, *Beautiful birds
Aren't they,* but there are none

To be seen snapping &
Popping like powerlines arcing

In an ice-storm. *They're
Yellow-tailed black cockatoos* (she
Says without looking back).

There a maybe seen flare
Of pale tail feathers,
Pinecones falling

Like fat fizzing
Raindrops on slate
Faster & then too a half

Dozen down in quick
Succession   swallowed

By vines & leaves
Fallen branches
A latticed floor.

yes

> *enough*
> *socks yes*
> *enough*
> *blanke**t**s*

not

> *allowed*
> *pants*
> *with ties no*
> *leggings*

no she

> *doesn't know when*
> *the nurses will*
> *message him*

yes

> *an egg*
> *& lettuce sandwich*
> *yogurt **a**nother*
> *girl got her*
> **green**
> *tea poured by*
> *a nurse*
> *there's no*
> *boiling water*
> *hanging*
> *around*
> *the ward*

no

> *not*
> *by*
> *the bed*
> *charging*
> *is only*

at a **table** outside
the nurse's
station

no

_______ not
for the first
morning
in a **long**
time

no

definitely
no knitting
needles
and
no

it's

quiet
one her age a few
in their 20s who
she talked to
when she arrived there's
nothing
that would lead
anyone to think
it's **an I**CU
_______ ward

they're

busy
doing paper
work will **wait** be
fore bothering them
about cord**s**
again

they're not

allowed
to leave this ward
it's **a** closed
ward

no you

can't
she has to
sign
some**th**ing
first you
can't

sh**e**

should
just come
home

(stand b**y**

the sink
after school week
ends window to
CFA car park
one car arrives
parks in a bay sometimes
with th**e** child**re**n sometimes
it's the one without
another car arrives
faster than the first and parks
imprecisely two or three bays over each
steps out meets roughly
in the middle
of the asphalt
followed
by children and

bags moving from one
car to the other the parents
gravitate towards the
departing car
beside which
they all for mo**re** or less time stand
before the car with the kids
leaves first
not
slowly)

she

should
just come
home

no not even

with masks
no one
you can't
not even
parents

not even

parents
no one you
can't not
even
with masks

Eyes strained, cheekbone pressed
to partly wound windows
of a moving car, past

paddocks crops abattoir
in your Catholic school-uniformed
casual-clothes day dread

fence line flashes
of holding yards of haysheds
dread

of the pastel-clad
Queensland holiday-tanned
girls, seated together

the Anglo big house
streets, smart side of the sixth-grade
classroom's graded desk

arrangement — its radial design its
skin-colour correlations — passing

the not-long opened
American-style shopping centre's
terracotta sprawl

along the signed stretch
of new & used cars, ticker-tape
snap of rainbow bunting

past VicRail's commuter train
going the other way, the running
late school-bound belt-free

backseat of small bodies
*but he's staring at me she
touched me he's right over*

myside the push shove & squall
of younger sister two younger
brothers, end of the free

sun-warmed one-third pint
bottles of mandatory mid-morning
milk (& conversion from

imperial measure)
towards the traffic-lit end
of a street's real and imagined

address, the *loony bin*
the *that place* the *funny farm*

the *insane asylum* the *nuthouse*
the *for the mad* the *mental*

the *bonkers* the *defectives*
the *away with the pixies* the

lunatics the *that's where they end
up alright,* air thin in the wake

of whichever never sure to which
ivory trimmed red-brick or bluestone
building his waved from the steering

wheel back of hand referred
runaway swallowed   over the throat
of you-knew-not-what but you did

know what if not after what
it was properly called that house
she'll bloody well get locked up in or

she should bloody well check into.
It was called and calls back now,

the hand not long and the house long gone.
It was called Dax House.

not

         their first
       admission so they
     had the good sense
      to bring a beanie
         to pull
      down over their
           eyes

maybe *she*

      *should re**a**d it it*
       doesn't look
    read like no one's ever
     read it the copy
    *on the coffee **table***
       of Anna
       Karenina

yes

          she
      remembers that

a joke

     because she could
       have ______
        (sewn /
  into the lining of her dress)
      she doesn't but
       she could
      and no one
      would know
       no one

______

            ______

but

          what

do **you** mean she
means how did you
know that anyway that
nurse doesn't
work here
anymore

yes

she is
safe
there

no

please
no she'd
rather you
didn't say
anything

you missed

her **call**
there**'s**
no message

yes

and
with an actual
door

no

not allowed
any
appliances
like
that

like she

was keeping him
by asking him

all these
questions
when

some

of them
barely come
once a week

are **you**

*t*hin

or

thick
skinned

some of them

barely
come once a week

if she

could she
would go outside
stand
in the wind

if she could

she'd **be** going
out**side**
to stand
(arms wrapped)
in *t*he wind

pulped tissues from the wet clothes
    food scraps from the drain
racket of utensils returned

to divided drawers and plates
    to other plates
the ticking dial ignites

a gas burner & the other
    child's leave-me-alone outrage —
(awake all night no not

online then Chelsea's penalty
    shootout loss) — hurls a small ball
at the framed Led Zeppelin

avocado without shattering
    morning grey flush
of sharp windowpane to face wet

tyres on bitumen braking
    bus engine's acceleration through
the roundabout whirr of heater

from beneath the desk in pleated
    dark the dog yelps underfoot soiled
rain clatters over corrugated

skylight falls the concrete length
    of the flooding patio like
so many loosely threaded

sewing machine needles,
     each unthreading drop
flaps up to hit the next,

and next the swollen
     seedpod over days bursts
its pink inflorescence, mop

of beaded locks loosening
     upward & flowering around,
pretty parasol hung

on the side of a spindle trunk
     stretching noon above the roof
by sodden suburban stairs, planted

as though this place were some
     lush place else, perfect
for the patriarchal monarch

of all palms — (which next year
     will fail to open
the full pod fallen

spilling
     its crimped strings
its dark
     desiccations)

older

with white
blonde hair scary
eyes doesn't
let them
hug each other even
on appropriate
occasions
like someone is leaving
for another ward or
someone is upset
in a contained
way
but that is more
understandable
than not letting them
walk

there's a bed

on a good unit
she's going
to miss it she's
not been
approved
for transfer he
won't come in
till late be gone
by then

no

those pants have ties
remember
no leggings
she

feels

like
she's too
*upset **to** do*
anything except
leave
she just wants
to leave

the other

strict nurse
is on she gets
mad when they
pace never mind they
are locked in
a tiny
ward
pacing
she

takes back

                what she said
         about cords it seems
         the only short cord she's
      managed to keep **hold of**
  is one that charges the charger
        not **an**y of the ones
            that allow her
        to charge her devices
              using that
                charger

with one

            of the **old** ladies
             in the ward
           it's the first Spanish
            conversation
             she's had since
              elementary
                school

TikTok

             yes she means
                 why
          do you ask that

she has

                 been
               moved
            to the _______
                ward

Tik-

                 Tok
                 yes
        she means why do you ask
                that

did

she say
she's not seen
any boys or
men here yet

she has

not seen
any boys or
men here yet

Dax
The (made in England)
Psychiatrist (1908–2008)
Of (modified) leucotomy and art therapy
Inaugural Chairman of the Mental Health
Hygiene Authority of Victoria (1952) replacing
The Department of Mental Hygiene (which replaced
The Lunacy Department) established under the provisions
Of the Mental Hygiene Authority Act 1950
Having issued from the Mental Hospitals Inquiry Committee (1948)
Into the reportedly overburdened Director of the Branch
And unreliable Public Service Board and Public Works Department
To recommend an independent board appointed by
The Governor-in-Council of three commissioners
Not subject to the provisions
Of the Public Service Act and reporting directly
To the Minister for Health to administer
The Mental Hygiene and the Mental
Deficiency Acts including responsibility
For the Mental Hygiene Branch
With   complete control
Though technically
The Secretary
Of the Department
Of Health had
Control over
The staff

she

                              tried
                      not to laugh
you

                           already
                          told her
                  his name she's
                           already
                              been
                             there
she's

                          allowed
                               now
                          to go to
                      the proper
                      dining hall
                     courtyard &
                           groups
no

                            it was
                        more like
                         a **free**
                           for all
she

                         was not
                             able
                 to make it up
              in time for that

                    he goes home
                      every week
                            for it
                               it's
for Shabbat

better than

an **a**dolescent
ward

but

there seems
no point in
staying
when

no

she has not
been able
to no she
cannot stay on
hold no there
is nobody
to email

one

of them
has three children
at home between
ag**e**s 6 & 11

she

feels she'd
be better
off at home
ch**ar**ge her own
devices run her own
art therapy

another

said
she lost
a twin in utero it
was the doctor's fault

they sued him she
*said he **destroyed** all*
his notes all
*the evid**en**ce now*
she sees him
driving around
South Yarra
in a white
Mercedes
SUV

here's

some of what
she did in
Sunday's
open art
studio

there's

a separate
list for that
she didn't get
her name down
in time for that

you already

said
that

you

already said that

soccer parent sideline
looks up in unison   eyes follow
the bubbling eastward motion

moving mass of screeching
pink & grey galahs high
overhead swiftly their pale

bellies passing above
the flood-lit oval to inky dark
night sky colour of cold

wind   of more virulent returns
dense muscular squelch of ball
to hear it coming   anything

true swiftly grows   around it
surrounds it   to keep the body safe
spell waving   detached ears in hands

laughter   loose elbows   scent
of sage   ears rolled about in oneiric
play with velvet equine lips

first the levity   the warm
waking drift   the merry
hypnopompic gift

then the shame of having
taken   a recently
read poem's

sorry sack
of executed
ears

it's not

what
she thinks
you imagine locked
doors long
antiseptic smell
*of **cor**ridors*
though the doors
are
sometimes locked
she said

can you add

*to yo**u**r list*
the grey long
***s**leeved*
one put her name
on the bag
leave it at
reception where
*they inspe**c**t*
everything
first

the court-

*ya**r**d*
they have to
ask to go
out in
is like
a miniature prison
yard
with cute
*pain**ting**s*
on the corrugated

iron

no

(petticoat

webbed
cream mole
skin circa
1910–1930
prior to
the use of sedatives
webbing a triangular
stitched section sewn together
back & front
ankle-length
hem to crotch
making
the wearer hobble
canvas shoulder straps
reinforced double
layer stitching
oblong open piece
running down back to below
waist secured by
horizontal straps
with screw-type
locking brass
buckles
across
the gap)

not

today
only
his registrar

came this
morning

no

she **like**s
the one
she started reading
yesterday

(by

the front door
a basket
of jasmine
purple pinwheels
curly parsley
rainbow chard)

or

try
the clear
spiral folder
tucked
at the bottom
left
of the desk
on the floor

she

said
in a not so subtle
or compliant way when
the nurse came in
to check on
her she wants
to discharge
herself to**day**

she

doesn't know why
they'd tell you that
that's not what
happened
it's not

happened then
why
would they
tell you
that

Dax
The House (1969)
Not to be mixed up with Baxter
The House (1954) next door
One for the *nutters*
One for the *knocked up*
Till Dax House one day stripped & reconstructed
The Baxter House maternity patients
Moved to Dax House & the Dax House psychiatric patients
Moved round the corner to the former Swanston Street Primary School
By which time the Mental Health Act 1959 had been repealed
By others of the same name different dates done up the decades
With the Australasian Association of Psychiatrists (1946)
Precursor to The Australian & New Zealand College
Of Psychiatrists (1963) with Royal prefix (1977) plus
A dash of the talking cure with rising pharmacopoeia &
The American Psychiatric Association's Diagnostic
And Statistical Manual of Mental Disorders first (1952)
Edition's one hundred pages into the next millennium
Another thousand pages five new editions & four text
Revisions (counting the 7th printing of DSM-II
Not called a Text Revision for dropping
Homosexuality as a listed disorder)
Arabic replacing Roman numerals
Decimals for incremental updates
Like software versioning though
DSM-5 with a TR anyway per
Past convention clusters of over-
Lapping signs to fugitive
Accord of systems absent
Of clear cause
Not guidelines for
Treatment not
For cure

no she

> > > *can't*
> > > *just*
> > > *check out*
> > > *any time she*
> > > *likes it's not*
> > > *a hotel*

given

> > > *the nurse*
> > > *had to ______*
> > > *the ______*
> > > *& the ______ for*
> > > *______ she thinks*
> > > *they're not going*
> > > *to let her no*
> > > **matter** *how*
> > > *persuasive*
> > > *she is*

they've called

> > > *him they've*
> > > *agreed if he*
> > > *ha***s** *not arrived*
> > > *by the time their*
> > > *sh***ift fin***ishes*
> > > *toni***g***ht*
> > > *she won't*
> > > *see him she*
> > > *needs*
> > > *sleep*

she doesn't know

> > > *she has no*
> > > ***idea***
> > > *what to do*
> > > *with*

with half

an hour's
worth
of song**s**
she

she knows

that
but you
did not r**espond**
to her
question
no

someone is

cleaning
her room
no

they

left
to de**f**end
their thesis
at
midday

she will

sort it
on**line**
she

maybe she

ha**s**
more imagination
than you
do

she thought she

had
replied to that

maybe she

likes
speculation
more *than you do*

that

*could ha**v**e been*
withdrawal this
could be
new side effects or
maybe
*someth**ing** else*

that

could have been
withdrawal this
could be
new side effects or
maybe
something else

TO SLIDE DOWN & STAND THERE
(DAX #4)

chopped lost into loosely
                                  diced
          yellow onion one halfmoon thumbnail
                                       when
     the other child calls out
                           to come see
         the last light's drizzling
                      rain turned   heavy
hail rousing a younger
          preschool   self grinning eye
              lashes speckled
scoops up in double handfuls
              fashions snow angels
                       with his bare
                            toes
smell Sunday's
   lamb roast
      next door
         the fish & chips shop
  over   the road drifts
      the car park   empties
          the elderly neighbours go
to bed and from her night
               kitchen
   your mother's
   Face-
  Time eyes
       stare
         a skipping
    beat

Why did you ask
that?

seeing not

the breezy lamp-lit

digressions from where

you'd led her

by

stable doors &

saddle racks by

windrowed crops bantam hens

the jersey cow

remember

those always mating

black & red

harlequin bugs

those chorusing crickets all

pouring

from the cracked '70s summer

ground

of Lara   then

closer

remember

Suzanne Silks   & Griffiths

Books

but

to it

plainly *What*

made you ask that?

& you brace

for your father

threatened

to check her   in

but   it doesn't come she

                                              wanted
              to go there she

                                        was ______

she was

                              a mess she was
                                 beside herself he
          hid   the car keys
                    would have been too embarrassed
to have   a wife
                                           in that place
               to have a wife who'd been in
                                          that place
        wouldn't want to be left
                                         with four small
                                            children
           well eventually she
                                       pulled
                                       herself

                together You
        were there
                       you
                                     must
                                      have known
and did you   know
                     her grandmother
                          your great-grandmother
          spent   her last decade
                                          somewhere
                    outside Auckland
                          dying young
        in one
        that's where they put them   then
                  for Huntington's

                              chorea

                                                    and *No*
she doesn't know
                         doesn't remember exactly
            where
            Dax House was
                         No

are you

                                        still
                                        there
today's

                                        roast
                                        beans **whi**te
                                        rice vegetab**le**s
                                        on the side zucchini
                                        pumpkin
                                        corn
now **drawing**

                                        in
                                        her room
tomorrow a group

                                        on _______
                                        & then **the**
                                        _______ group
also nail polish

                                        remover
                                        and that
                                        old Spanish
                                        grammar
                                        book
today's

                                        was calle**d**
                                        Art
                                        In
                                        A Circle
                                        about
                                        drawing
                                        your feelings
                                        in
                                        a circle

no

masks no
one is
wearing them
much this
time

you mean

what she's
listening to
right now
you would
not have heard of them
she said

even some of the **nurses**

laugh
in **the** *last*
few days
some review's
going on so they're
already
following
protocol
to
a tee

a cool

nurse
just **said**
Nice curly locks
as he
passed by
doing one of
the night
checks

(white

                                     canvas
                                     locked
                                     glove
                                circa 1910
                           pear-shaped mitten
                            with wrist strap
                    brass buckle with small
                          torpedo-shaped
                                screw-in
                            bolt turned
                             with key)

she hates the way

                           other people just
                                      use
                            those words
                              (to dull
                          the sawtooth
                              edges)

please

                           don't ask that

(don't ask

                                    that)

HIDDEN MOTHER PHOTOGRAPHY

Not looking directly
but skirting the edges,
more and more pretending

to arrive eventually
like your mother manoeuvring
backwards a skittish pony

into the vet crush it baulked
at walking into face first, each
response and inquiry

immaculate emulsion of patience
& despair, shrieking silence
of an easy miscibility, upright

and insensible, clawing itself back
from purchased displacement only
to land on a wash of maternal

refusal, wild limbs hung limp while
uncertainly seen lightning cracks
flare into proleptic broadsheet

though you once lived really lived
with each of them & still, this
neither the vaunted letting go nor

hanging on, the thing gone wild gone
rogue gone bush gone wrong, hidden
behind a curtain under a cloak

disguised as a chair a tear
in the collodion, mother
as abecedarian, keep

the farrier booked rugs
on the stalls mucked
the grain and chaff bins

full, no one
is being spelled
for the winter

yes

she's
still here

look on

the floor there
or under the bed it's there
a short cord
some
where

yes

you can
even with
the door closed
you can
can you
wait **while**
she sees if she
can go out
to the courtyard
to call you

(a rusted

'68
Holden ute
sitting beneath a loft
its back half
on blocks
fit for purpose
whose other purpose
was long past
axle driving
the black rubber conveyor
belt turning a wheel turning
the blades deafening

roar and dust
storm of it all
bellow & holler
kids in muddled height
splitting oaten
sheaves shredding
lucerne bales to biscuits
her pushing it down
the *narrowing*
chute to
him stuffing it
towards the grinding
maw snatched unstoppable
cut chaff
yellow or green
flying out the other end her
running back and forth
to unhook move replace
the filled hessian sacks later sewn
shut everyone's heavy green
or yellow snot
handkerchiefed
& long
creased cries
of muck
in eyes)

one

hour
of unescorted
leave he gave her
tomorrow she
can get coffee
*by her***self**

to one of the

nurses about
her concerns about
Dr A. she
says she should
try to get
a second
o**pinion**
she should
talk to th**e**
hea**d**
nurse who'll be in
tomorrow
when

no

not
anymore
that **regist**rar
would b**e**
a **r**eal
psychiatri**st**
now

with

the vaping
in the carpark
in **the** dark
with **order**ed pizzas
group

no

not any
of those the
opposite
in

bed
can't
be
*bothe**red***
***mov**ing*
can't

_____

_____

she knows

she

yes she's still

*you ar**e***

knows

here

FROM EVERYWHERE

green's understorey, the tangled
                trail ends above timberless
      expanse of shallow river flooding

vast rocky slopes fast moving
                rapids tumbling ivory lace sight
      dilates ready to move with it

away down-hill but odd the eyes
                will not declare it stare at it
      wither and sink back to see

the water moves up-hill gathering
                ground towards what plea when
      over the surface travelling

on a faster clear frictionless conveyance
                comes glassy comes tall-jointed
      appendages of one then

another step-gliding trans-
                lucent arthropods streaming
      to the top abrupt cut away

vanishing edgeways, to a trickling vent,
                out of sight,
      found shoe-box remains, for no

decent reason inventoried,
                the old pink & red re-assembled
      IKEA top drawer jumble:

twisted Silly Bandz Pearler Beads Women's
                World Cup swap cards pieces of Polly
        Pocket paperclip purple velvet

hair ribbon red gel pen Lorde CD liner
                battery-less headlamp three
        marbles clear lip gloss leather bracelet blue

feather Matchbox race car bouncy ball ball
                of steel-grey wool Lamorinda
        key ring one US one-dollar note

snap of green & yellow
                budgerigar left
        behind once-dogeared *(Smart*

Girls Guide To) Liking
                Herself—Even on the Bad
        Days empty brown bottle of Bach's

Rescue Remedy Sleep
                Drops not empty
        blister pack of Strepsils

to break
                and remake
        it otherwise

it

                                  was
                      *good **to** be out*
                            in the rain
                                 (light)

she doesn't know

                                 wen
                  *he'll come wor**r**ies*
                             it won't be
                                *tod**a**y*
                                 *th**e**n*

a semester

                                   off
                         ***g**raduating*
                                 must
                       *have **lo**cked*
                          *hims**e**lf in*
                        the bathroom
                           the nurses
                               asking
                              Do you
                      have ______
                             ***i**n there*
                   *he mus**t** have he*
                            just left
                            with two
                          paramedics

and earlier when

                                   she
                    was lonely she
                        met a friend

who's now **in** the ______

unit and they

drank **tea**

in her

gr**o**up area

instead

(breaking

mid

night after night

over any

volume of white

noise like avian

slaughter

which heard

fin**a**lly

from the backyard

was high

in the lemon

gum next door

the discordant screeching

of one

creature)

a s**pe**cial

dinne**r**

did

you make

one

also

her cream cord

flares

& la**ce**-u**p**

boots

some

times
but
not always
*access**ible***

pacing

up
& down
her room
she took
it much later
when she
should
have taken it
to stop
pacing
now she
doesn't know
*what **she**'s*
doing
when

(early 17th-

century
instruction
for the melancholic
looks like
21st-century's
self-care & wellness
without
*the **cap**italism)*

no she

                              doesn't
                         want that
                         she can't

a few of the nurses

                         and even
                one of the doctors
                       have asked
                  what she was like
          when she was young was
                she _______ or _______
                    was she _______
                         as a child

what

                was she like when
             she was young was
                she _______ or _______
                    was she _______
                         as a child
                    even a doctor
                           a few
                    of the nurses

THE OTHER HOSPITAL

Along the rocky sides of the school-
run road wild purple-throated
freesias white bushland weeds
environmental hazard happily spread
to the not-seen before bloodshot
patch of them breezy spreading
bright red splotch of them
un-owned un-attested sweet un-
claimed excess of them, there's no
absorbing & anyway no
ignoring occasional arboreal
claims out the closed car window,
another season just blew by,
the not-yet days unfurl on repeat
on loop it plays again on do it again
on nothing is happening again
on this is not helping again

At the cafe's coffee window
to a strollered child's ascendant
cry, picture pages flapping
as the cast-off book had landed
like a sagging tent spine up, quickly
bending the grandmother had sung *There
was an old man named Michael
Finnegan he had dah-dah dah-dah
dadada* falling to this then to
this can't we do it over again *a-
long came the wind & dah-dah
dadada* midnight-blue eyes unblinking

home from the other hospital baby
capsule back of taxi front of
Mount Sinai, there's no beginning
again, *poor old dah-dah dadada*

Begin-agen, on repeat on loop it
plays again on do it again, home
from the other hospital
midnight-blue eyes unblinking
no nursing & sleeping and
waking & nursing   no
blent milky beginnings this tree
that flower that cloud this light
cry, *poor old dah-dah dadada,*
dog pees again, on the carpet
of the other child's bedroom,
is put out returns skid
marks across the living room mat
to resume its post watching
the street, still, for its mistress's
return, handyman leans against
the sun-streaked laundry door
quietly scrolling replacement hinges
for the scraping gate
when the other child texts
he feels _______ & cannot _______
blew them in-a-gain last night's
birthday candles

she still

needs you
to bring her her
sandals

no she'd

rather
talk about it
on the phone
another
day

but after

he
asked if she
were in
a relationship
listen to this
he asked
Men
Women
she was not
expecting that

the eye

mask
it never passed
inspection

they

take them
to **the** dog park
they can just walk
around but to**day**
a few people
were running
so tomorrow morning

during the walk
she's going
to run

(your

diligently
diagrammed
teenage cursive
falls from last
century's
brittle pages lost
longing
for continuance
instruction
announcing
again
the diagonal aids
whatever
the inside leg
produces
the outside hand
balances whatever
the outside leg supports for
bending & impulsion
the inside hand
sustains)

are you

busy can
you come
take her on
leave maybe go
for
a walk
then

at

five
days old
it died

you have

no idea
how your help
is the wrong
help

sorry

she missed
your calls

until

her fingers
and toes
were stiff
the nurses **begged** *her*
to take ______
until

there's

a long
list
to *use it she*
has no
clean under
wear

until her

fingers & toes
were stiff the nurses
begged her
to take ______
until

you can't

expect her
*to **an**swer that*

you can't expect

her
*to **answer***
that

TRAVEL BOARD GAMES

Small enough to slip
In any handbag   three-in-one
For all ages family fun

Folds up no mess no fuss snaps
Shut   keeps all pieces in
Place compact & packable

Vacation essential
Little magnetic little half-
Life travel board games of grief   play

If you had tried to _______   if you
Had been more ______ and more present

To ______   if when she ______ you
Had not ______   if when she ______ you

Should have ______   if you'd done that if
______ had not happened there

Would not be ______ and she would
Have ______ and none   of this

Would have happened he can't
Hear that you can't say that

To him   falls funnelling floors
Slam of slamming doors there's no

Looking any of this up
In a book   old glory days
Of sight-seeing ease

What was on offer   *Your _____ Child*
The _____ Child   Raising a _____ Child
Living With Your _____ Child

Their creased spines shelved tight behind
The armchair there from where
You might   admire again

Your new yellow mug
The made somewhere-not-around-here mug
Yellow ceramic mug could buy

Matching plates (more cups) or bowls then
Wonder how   you've not seen that before
The *high time you begin to collect*

Old blue china three thousand pieces of which
Will leave you bankrupt   Mary Ruefle's
Menopause manifesto

A tiny room of no-one-else's   part
Coffin (Mrs Dalloway's narrow bed)   part
Prairie (Antonia's Nebraska)

Tiny room for not imagining anything
Else but what else you've already
Seen   then wonder

How you've not seen this before
Stock standard
Of your frightened figurations

Your failed flights from
The sight of what you cannot unsee the sight
Of how many ways a person can

Protest   never mind these trees
Are simply living   gums with gaping

Glyptic copper marks precisely
Scored one-half dozen
Horizontal lines

Of cicatrice   gums with charred
Burls drizzling seals

Of crimson ooze blade-thin
Russet lenticels   a scribbly gum's
Pyrography pen the box

Elder's scorched flags
Of final assertions   for which

What could that mother do?
Their mother Clymene who was too
Late   poplar bark wrapping

Around already closing
Over the Heliades' last words last

Calls for her   their hair into leaves
Torsos to trunks   limbs boughs
What can their mother do

But try to save them?
Tears turn to resin as each
Vanishing child torn   cries out

To be spared
The further injury of her misguided effort
To do something   to do

Something   anything
Else but what else you've already

Done   to find your thin song

A small wattle tree
August laden yet upright   ply

Of soft percussive threads
Making which it is   of wattles

Gossamer golden weeping   wattles
Prickly velvet star-leaved
Creeping   wattles box-leaved coastal

Wedge-leaf orange-wreathed
Red-leaf flax-leaf   most
Grown

Leaves not leaves
But phyllodes

like

she
didn't
want
to get up
and try again
she's
sorry

(un

til
she is not
safe t
here)

it

was
her choice

no

she
didn't
leave
a message

what

is PBS
they *said it's not*
in
PBS

yes

she asked if
he could
take her on
long **term** *he*
sounded
surprised he
said Oh
I'm only in
my rooms every
three or four
weeks
but telehealth
three days
a week very
busy but
sure

at home

how is
everyone

(through

the
vertical
gap
between
hotel
window frame & blind
angular

sheets
***of** car light*
up from the street slide
open over
the bed folding
night back on
itself)

she

talked to her
after dinner for
ages she
was born in
Egypt
just before WWII
*she **speak**s French*
Arabic
Italian
Greek

still

next
Thursday
though possibly
*stay**ing***
for art therapy
first

she

was born
in Egypt
just before WWII
she speaks French
Arabic
Italian
Greek

some of them

it's just that they
have nowhere else
to go

some of them

it's just that
they have
nowhere
else
to go

ANYWAY

After sitting like any other
of many mothers fully
dressed beside the turned away
back of the child in bed, or
standing outside that bedroom's door
or, sitting or sleeping on that bedroom floor

as any other of many mothers
who might have rathered the blame
still be cast like it used to be
wholly in-house than locked away
in that child's brain, having
rolled already rolled anyway

beneath the pharmacy's
late-night lights through
childhood's breakages, you
retreat, not knowing
long rippling lines of back-
burn low flame arcing across

yellow hills of dry grass from
prescribed lines of indecipherable
script tiny orange-fired loops & curls
and either way smoke skeins scatter
your chest trips a nervous streak
wakes throatfuls of *I am terribly*

sorry over and over eyes over
sodden deck planks falls one way *I
am terribly sorry* rises another *I am*

terribly sorry treble stepping
over the same subsiding
terrain *(for my messy the mess*

this mess) needs blue hair & yellow
curly-toed shoes, marionette
with a pencil for a nose,
a sonic Mr Squiggle
to fill in the blanks of what nobody
knows, while she is anyway

here living it her one
life at its bearable limit

are you able

to check wait lists
again

she tried she asked all

her direct questions
today
when

he told her to go further

afield
from hospital
tomorrow see how
she feels

when she tried to **tell** him

she'd felt _____
had been getting _____ he
told her it must
be _____ she
doubts he
has ever had _____ or felt
_____ before

(when

                                           tall
                                   rectangular
                                       blocks
                                    of vertical
                                 rain cloud one
                                     at a time
                                         fall
                just as a high-rise a sky
                    scraper collapses
                                   directly
                                 into its own
                                 footprint
                                   falling
                               recurrent
                                 from left
                                 to right
                          from where you
                                   stood)

no she would sign

                                 herself out
                                     then
                      come *to meet you*

no you

                                     didn't
                         see **a** *missed*
                                       call

from Tumblr

                         then no one said
                                 anything
                                 to How
                         does it make you
                                   feel

so after a while
the therapist said
Well
does anyone know
a poem
and
no one else
volunteered
so
she found
on her phone Prufrock
read *out*
bits **of** *it she*
remembered *from school*
no one said
much
so
in the end
a very
short
session

just Copic fine **line**rs *from*

the desk drawer

in

the news
did you
read it

she'll be **waiting**

at reception you're
allowed **in**to
the foyer
with a mask

in the newspaper

                                    did you read it

the room who is

                                            in
                                the room with you

(who is in the room with

                                    you)

CLOSED WARD ADMISSIONS

To get your child in there to keep her in there, later
                     to get her out of there to keep her out of there

Keep it all within reach, the unforeseen the frightful
                     all its variations, not then but now

You find again that mother's face
                     fixed by the newspaper picture, you

Think of her addressability, her funereal black, you
                     try to think of these months of her mourning

But blankly picture yourself picturing yourself
                     picturing her again & again, not

Now but later you see you did not see
                     her eyes meet, squarely, the public

Camera's, your hand cast
                     across the private page, to get

Your child in there to keep her in there, later
                     to get her out of there to keep her out of there

yes you do remember

William William Henry Stephen
Henry Richard John oi
you
remember
that's all
the English
kings and queens
since William first
that there have been

you know

from that show
Horrible
Histories
they used to watch
when they
were little there's
a board game
Stupid Deaths
one of the doctors
*gave it to one **of** his patients*
to see

if it wasn't too
triggering
Will
You Get
The Grim Reaper
or
Will
The Grim Reaper
Get You
they all
found it hilarious
so it passed
the test

yes a different

doctor
he'll be
seeing her
now until
the end of her
admission Dr A.
has Covid

mostly he agreed

with him
about
what
happened she

she still

has no
access
to any of
her things
except what
she needs

right
now

opposite

the nurse's
station
so light
coming
through
the curtains
all night

yes

he's
not
president of
or president of
or honorary member of
anything

please

tell her
you're
okay
tell her

she's

sorry she
missed
your calls
she is
okay now

please

don't
cry
all the way
home

                                              (it
                                            peels
                                            away
                                         easy as
                                          paper)

          last night was

                                           rough
                                       but today
                                        morning
                                           group
                                      is with the
                                         seniors

          last night

                                      was rough
                                but morning group
                                         is with
                                    the seniors
                                          today

INSTITUTIONAL CHOREOGRAPHIES

The parents wait here
    there the doctor enters, scree
        of a fully enclosed windowless

hospital consultation room,
    supposing good footing good
        shoes right direction all

and none of that for secure
    laughs *Oh no no of course*
        windows on the third floor

do not open but heard not
    heard for laughs there four feet up
        on the windowsill to a ground

three floors below *Hello*
    there what-are-you-doing-up-there
        the nurse's softly amused

voice for toddlers cutely not yet
    asleep, but what of that afternoon
        leave that tracked down city streets

eve of All Hallows' Eve gold-
    cased crystal black Gucci
        lipstick, the last black lipstick

left anywhere, anyway not worn
    wishing dead lips lacquered
        for an ICU-skipped trick

or treat, then when the un-
    flinching the collapsing lopsided
        orographic lifting is over *(Ah*

the carpet here's the same as at
    the office), the brief-cased
        psychiatrist in his smiley baggy

way rises from the table
    walks them to the elevator *Ah yes*
        well, yes durable I s'pose — spaces

habitable by the bodies
    shaping them, it's slow to see
        harder to hold, her daughter died

from a differential what
    of what keeps yours alive,
        institutional choreographies

of colonial white, wobbly dripping
    streams of red tail-lights braking peak
        hour Punt Road to Hoddle Street

flash of blue siren light rolling
    catty-cornered digital billboards throb
        whiskey watches services streaming white

plastic bags blown wet beside lit
    petrol station stretches of freeway
        while the Trojan women

irritatingly wail within earshot
        What was it all for? (their
            protection privilege their lineage

lost), this your self-pity note you
        gave your child life but not the
            (dada-dah) desire to keep it

no it doesn't

work that way

———

———

(nothing works

to

day)

no she's been distracted watching

with her friend
the last few hours this
other patient
screaming
at the nurses she
threatened
to discharge herself they
salvaged **all the flowers** she'd
thrown in the bin
on the way out
now they
each have
nice b**ou**quets
in their
rooms

yes you have

they're in
most of her flower
(burning
flower)
drawings

if tomorrow Dr B. and

the nurses she
values their opinion
more think leaving

on the weekend

is a good

idea then Sunday

morning

(passing in

to road

side view another

Grevillea's

golden

plates

float

like a distant temple's edged ex

travagance

exceeding the contents

of those same horizontal limbs

bleached in

to the glistering

hillside haze)

no because ______ was only just

approved for

treatment of ______

can you see if they

are with

the **black rose**

*earring**s***

small box same

cabinet

no she does not want

you to come help her

pack

that's

not what

*sh**e** sai**d***

that's not what she

                              meant

no she

                    did **not**
                get through all
                 the discharge
                paperwork
about that he said

                          just
                    Let's wait
                       & see
you missed a call

                    but the caller
              didn't leave a message
she spent hours with her

                    this evening her
            brain now merrily glitching
                    in multiple
                    languages
she spent **hours** this evening merrily
                    in multiple languages

WAITING

Not even high leaves.
Not the sickle-shaped leaves
beyond the back fence, not
last year's leaves marcescent

by the shed fence, scent
of jonquil muddy rain boots
back door of a dead friend's house.
Not this dread stillness not this.

Allow me the kicked back
clod of wet grassy paddock
as metal horseshoes fly
by. Even riderless even

just the smell. Still
not a single peel of curling
bark not a single leaf falls,
not even a thin wave.

Atop the bamboo screen
the miner bird sits (ache
of iatrogenic mis-
steps) does not hop down

hops further away hops
up to the telephone
wire and away, waiting
for new editions any

decremental reversals
or revisions to forever
and always waiting
for what might or might not

come to pass be
looked back upon
as the problem the source
the moment the thing.

Unchecked the algorithmic rest
glides by in glinting digital
light blooming identificatory
desires, requisite faces

assemble closed-mouthed
bereft stiff pouts
of pursed lips
passing as smiles.

Beloved tree's broken
leaves buffeted and beaten
to one side silver
elastic skeleton of trunk

and branch tumbling flashes
of chipped blue sky high
in gunmetal-grey wind what I
want I want a thousand

years of care repair
of loose-rein returns

the remedy the correction
the counter-poison, a thousand

years of galloping in clear sky
half-light after the end
of whatever took
the daylight.

Through a blue mountain
valley of flannel flowers
dawn sweeps
printing

a fretwork of leaves
across a bare
wall, waiting for
nothing.

———

you'll both laugh

                                    at this
                              her friend
                         taught her this
                          great Italian
                               phrase
        Mi stai rompendo la testa

                       you're breaking
                           my head

literally

———

drawing

in her
room
(petals not petals
but
petal-like
bracts
soft
like ear lobes
downy like
sage
leaves)

it only helps

while
she's doing it

———

it

———

helps

AN ERASURE

13   a room all eyes

19   a room
to stop to
sleep to know
the mess
to bother
to take
all you need
of love

25   at a green
table long
and quiet
an I
waits
to leave a sign they
were there

32   maybe
a table
you know you
miss
calls you to come stand
beside it

37   to leave
the hold of an old
conversation

42   free to make
a garden

47   coruscating
      like rainbows tucked
      at the bottom
      of the day

52   matter
      sifting ideas
      despond of mid
      lines moving

59   while
      drawing the body
      time nurses
      the already
      said

64   while the self pinioned
      registers
      the order of
      remove

70   to wrangle it
      into
      a perceptible
      shape

76   the day begged
      to wear an answer

84   to leave
      the terms of speaking

90   tell me
      a tread

of remembered lines
waiting
in the foyer

95   of precarity

102   all the flowers
our black roses
packed in paper hours

NOTES

7   The epigraph, by C.D. Wright, is an excerpt from 'A Reader for Every Writer,' from *The Poet, the Lion, Talking Pictures, El Farolito, a Wedding in St. Roch, the Big Box Store, the Warp in the Mirror, Spring, Midnights, Fire & All,* (Washington: Copper Canyon Press, 2016). Copyright © 2015 by C. D. Wright. Reprinted with permission of The Permissions Company, LLC on behalf of Copper Canyon Press, coppercanyonpress.org.

13   The typographical presentation of the self-erasure text draws on Jen Bervins' erasure of Shakespeare's sonnets, *Nets,* (New York: Ugly Duckling Press, 2017).

15   The italicised lines in 'Listing' are from the title and final lines of the children's book by Doreen Cronin, *Click, Clack, Moo: Cows That Type,* (New York: Simon & Schuster, 2000).

17   "Split-flap display" boards are also known after the Italian manufacturer as Solari boards.

31   Dax House was a psychiatric hospital in Geelong, Victoria, which opened in 1969, was absorbed as a unit into Geelong Hospital in 1979 and into community mental health services in the 1990s.

32   The line "sewn / into the lining of her dress" is from Anne Sexton, 'Flee On Your Donkey,' *Mercies: Selected Poems,* (London: Penguin Books, 2020).

41   'Dax #2' includes language borrowed and adapted from the Public Record Office of Victoria, an archive of the State and Local Government, https://prov.vic.gov.au/archive/VA2838.

For the art collection housed at the Dax Centre, in Parkville, Victoria, see https://www.daxcentre.org, and Belinda Robson, *Recovering Art: A History of the Cunningham Dax Collection,* (Parkville: The Cunningham Dax Collection, 2006).

45   The final stanzas of 'When Tuesday Night's' refers to Carolyn Forché's poem 'The Colonel,' set on the eve of civil war in El Salvador, (1979–1992), *The Country Between Us,* (Northumberland: Bloodaxe Books, 1981).

48   The parenthetical lines borrow and adapt language from descriptions of two items held in the Psychiatric Services Collection, at Museums Victoria Collections, https://collections.museumsvictoria.com.au/items/269607, and https://collections.museumsvictoria.com.au/items/269605.

55   The title of the poem 'To Slide Down & Stand There' is from Rosmarie Waldrop, 'Conversation 3 On Vertigo,' *Gap Gardening: Selected Poems,* (New York: New Directions, 2016).

This poem is in memory of Christina Emma Jane Adam, (1904-1963).

57   Kingseat Hospital was a psychiatric hospital in Papakura, New Zealand, in operation 1932–1999.

61   The parenthetical lines borrow and adapt language from description of an item held in the Psychiatric Services Collection, at Museums Victoria Collections, https://collections.museumsvictoria.com.au/items/249301.

The phrase "to dull the sawtooth edges" is from William Styron, *Darkness Visible: A Memoir of Madness,* (New York: Vintage Books, 1992).

62   The title of the poem 'Hidden Mother Photography' refers to a 19th-century form of portraiture common with babies and young children, which conceals the mother's body as she supports the child to remain upright and still for the long exposure times. Forms of concealment include draping dark fabric, cropping, scraping or painting the emulsion.

63   The phrase "a tear in the collodion" is used by Laura Larson in her 13 June 2018 *Aperture* interview with Carmen Winant, about Larson's adoption memoir, *Hidden Mother,* (Baltimore: Saint Lucy Books, 2017). https://aperture.org/editorial/Hidden-mothers/.

70   W.S. Merwin, 'Rain Light,' *The Shadow of Sirius,* (Washington: Copper Canyon Press, 2008).

72   The parenthetical lines refer to Robert Burton, *Anatomy of Melancholy,* 1621, (Project Guttenberg, 2004).

77   The parenthetical lines adapt language from Franz Mairinger, *Horses Are Made To Be Horses,* (Adelaide: Rigby Press, 1983).

81   The italicised "high time you begin to collect old blue china three thousand pieces of which will leave you bankrupt" is from Mary Ruefle's prose poem 'Pause,' *My Private Property,* (Seattle: Wave Books, 2016).

82   The italicised lines on this and on the following page are from Ovid's *Metamorphosis,* Book II: "What could that mother do" is the translation by Mary M. Innes (London: Penguin Books, 1955); "What can their mother do" the translation by Stephanie McCarter (New York: Penguin Books, 2022).

85 PBS refers to the Pharmaceutical Benefits Scheme, which gives subsidised access to specific medications.

89 Mr Squiggle is the titular character from the ABC children's television series, (1959–1999).

95 The non-italicized lines are from 'The Monarchs' Song (English Kings and Queens),' in the BBC Children's series *Horrible Histories,* (BBC DVD Series 3, 2009).

98 The line "it peels away easy as paper" is from 'Face Lift,' *Sylvia Plath Collected Poems,* (London: Faber and Faber, 1981). Reproduced with the kind permission of Faber and Faber Ltd.

99 The title of the poem 'Institutional Choreographies' is from Michelle Fine's phrase "institutional choreography," 'Witnessing Whiteness,' *Off White: Readings on Race, Power and Society,* (New York: Routledge, 1997).

100 The third through fifth stanzas on this page are indebted to Sara Ahmed's analysis of racialised bodies in institutional spaces, 'A Phenomenology of Whiteness,' *Feminist Theory,* 8(2), 2007.

101 The speaker's mishearing adapts "all nothing, all for nothing," Euripides, *The Women of Troy,* translation by Don Taylor, (Methuen Drama: London, 2007).

102 "[B]urning flower" is from Alice Notley, *The Descent of Alette,* (New York: Penguin, 1992).

107 About the flannel flower, see Frances Bodkin, 'Talara'tingi – How the Flannel Flower came to be,' *D'harawal Dreaming Stories,* (Sussex Inlet: EnviroBook, 2019); also at https://dharawalstories.files.wordpress.com/2015/05/talaratingi1-2mb.pdf.

ACKNOWLEDGEMENTS

Slipstream was written on the unceded lands of the Wurundjeri
people of the Kulin Nation.

I would not have written this book without the years (and years)
of listening to and reading along with two podcasts: David
Naimon's 'Between the Covers: Conversations with Writers in
Fiction, Non-Fiction & Poetry'; and Rachel Zucker's 'Commonplace:
Conversations with Poets (and other people).' Thank you. I am also
grateful to the Community of Writers, in California, for the Writers'
Annex Online.

To Felicity Plunkett for her close reading, to Susan Le for cover
and book design, and Ralph Wessman, at Walleah Press, for
publication, many thanks.

To friends and family, thank you, for your company and love.
And, for everything, to Hannah and Raphael.

AUTHOR

Kristyn J. Saunders lives in Melbourne, Australia. She holds degrees from Deakin and Harvard Universities and a PhD in English & Comparative Literature, from Columbia University. This is her first book of poetry.

www.ingramcontent.com/pod-product-compliance
Lightning Source LLC
Chambersburg PA
CBHW032019180726
48283CB00008B/2748